TRANSCENDING RACE IN AMERICA
BIOGRAPHIES OF BIRACIAL ACHIEVERS

ALICIA KEYS

TRANSCENDING RACE IN AMERICA
BIOGRAPHIES OF BIRACIAL ACHIEVERS

Halle Berry

Mariah Carey

Derek Jeter

Alicia Keys

ALICIA KEYS

SINGER-SONGWRITER, MUSICIAN, ACTRESS, AND PRODUCER

Russell Roberts

Mason Crest

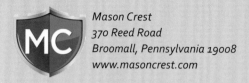

Mason Crest
370 Reed Road
Broomall, Pennsylvania 19008
www.masoncrest.com

Printed and bound in the United States of America.

First printing
9 8 7 6 5 4 3 2 1

Library of Congress Cataloging-in-Publication Data

Roberts, Russell, 1953-
 Alicia Keys : singer-songwriter, musician, actress, and producer / Russell Roberts.
   pages cm. – (Transcending race in America : biographies of biracial achievers)
 Includes index.
 Previously published: Alicia Keys / Russel Roberts. Broomall, Pa. :
 ISBN 978-1-4222-2727-5 (hardback) – ISBN 978-1-4222-1605-7 (series hardback) –
 ISBN 978-1-4222-9986-9 (ebook)
 1. Keys, Alicia--Juvenile literature. 2. Singers–United States–Biography–Juvenile literature.
 3. Rhythm and blues musicians–United States–Biography–Juvenile literature. 4. Racially mixed
 people–United States–Biography–Juvenile literature. I. Title.
 ML3930.K39R64 2013
 782.42164092--dc23
 [B]
                    2012028938

Publisher's notes:
All quotations in this book come from original sources, and contain the spelling and grammatical inconsistencies of the original text. The websites mentioned in this book were active at the time of publication. The publisher is not responsible for websites that have changed their addresses or discontinued operation since the date of publication. The publisher will review and update the website addresses each time the book is reprinted.

TABLE OF CONTENTS

"I HAVE BROTHERS, SISTERS, NIECES, NEPH-EWS, UNCLES, AND COUSINS, OF EVERY RACE AND HUE, SCATTERED ACROSS THREE CONTINENTS, AND FOR AS LONG AS I LIVE, I WILL NEVER FORGET THAT IN NO OTHER COUNTRY ON EARTH IS MY STORY EVEN POSSIBLE."

"WE MAY HAVE DIFFERENT STORIES, BUT WE HOLD COMMON HOPES.... WE MAY NOT LOOK THE SAME AND WE MAY NOT HAVE COME FROM THE SAME PLACE, BUT WE ALL WANT TO MOVE IN THE SAME DIRECTION—TOWARDS A BETTER FUTURE...."

—BARACK OBAMA, 44TH PRESIDENT OF THE UNITED STATES OF AMERICA

CHAPTER

1

As I Am Is Super

On June 24, 2008, 27-year-old Alicia Keys showed audiences at the BET Awards why her latest album, *As I Am*, had become another in a string of hit records. She also demonstrated the talent that had won her so many awards that *Billboard* magazine ranked her at number eighty among the top-100 artists of all time.

Music superstar Alicia Keys proudly holds her award for Best Female R&B Artist backstage at the 2008 BET Awards. That night she showed the range of her talent as she performed hit songs from the 1990s and was honored for the amazing success of her album *As I Am*.

A PERSONAL RECORD

That night, Alicia performed the hit song "Teenage Love Affair" from *As I Am*. (*Rolling Stone* magazine rated the song twenty-third among the top-100 songs of 2007.) She also displayed her range and appreciation of other **genres** of

Alicia's album, *As I Am*, showed fans a new direction in her music and was praised by critics. The *New York Times* commented, "*As I Am* radiates not just confidence but also experience," while *People* magazine noted that Alicia "continues to scale artistic heights."

music by performing several hit R&B (rhythm and blues) songs from the 1990s with the songs' original artists, such as TLC and En Vogue. It was no surprise that she was awarded the Best Female R&B Artist that night.

Even before the BET Awards, Alicia had already enjoyed several months of extraordinary success thanks to *As I Am*. **Introspective** and personal, the album marked another step on the ladder of Alicia's artistic development. She acknowledged how the album signaled a new direction for

BETting On Success

In 2001, to recognize the achievements of minorities in fields such as entertainment and sports, the Black Entertainment Television Network established the BET Awards. Alicia has won the award for the Best Female R&B Artist three times—in 2005, 2008, and 2010. She also won for Best New Artist in 2002.

The award the performers receive is based on three words: aspire, ascend, and achieve. The numerous categories for the musical performing arts include R&B, gospel, and hip-hop artists. As of 2011, Beyoncé was the most-nominated artist.

One of the most **prestigious** categories is the Lifetime Achievement Award. Past winners include Al Green, Diana Ross, Gladys Knight, and James Brown.

Another notable category is the Humanitarian Award. Previous winners of the Humanitarian Award include Don Cheadle, Quincy Jones, Danny Glover, and Muhammad Ali.

THE NEW RENAISSANCE

UPTOWN

THE STYLE ISSUE

FALL 2007

42 BLACK MASTERS YOU SHOULD KNOW

FALL FASHION VINTAGE CHIC

RIDIN' HIGH CARS THAT MAKE YOU GO VROOM

INSIDE UPTOWN'S HOUSE OF STYLE

PARTYING WITH A PURPOSE RUSH PHILANTHROPIC

THE REBIRTH OF ALICIA KEYS

+

DIANA ROSS
SWIZZ BEATZ
GRACE JONES
JUNE AMBROSE

EXPLORING TOKYO

Alicia's beauty and poise have been evident since she first burst onto the music scene. Her music awards and charity work have made fans want to see more of her. As a result, she has made numerous appearances on magazine covers and television programs.

her. "It definitely marks a new chapter. With this album, it was all about my own personal self-awareness."

Released in mid-November 2007, *As I Am* had been a sensation from the beginning. It sold 742,000 copies in its first week of issue. Just ten hours after the album's first single, "No One," had been sent to radio stations, it became one of the fastest-moving and highest-charting singles on the *Billboard* Hot R&B/Hip-Hop song list. At the end of the year, *Rolling Stone* ranked the record among the top-fifty albums of 2007. Even though it was released late in the year, the record was 2007's fourth best-selling album.

As I Am Continues to Shine

As the new year arrived, *As I Am* picked up momentum. Early in January, the RIAA (Recording Industry Association of America), which tracks record sales, certified the album triple platinum, which means it has sold over one million copies.

At the Grammy Awards on February 10, 2008, Alicia and her single "No One" received more honors—Best Female R&B Vocal Performance and Best R&B Song. Alicia once again demonstrated her comfort with different musical styles and eras. She opened the show by singing a duet with a video image of Frank Sinatra on his song "Learnin' the Blues."

Critical reception to *As I Am* had been strong. Fox News said that the record contained "some brilliant music," while the *New York Times* called it her "strongest effort yet." It was an excellent reception for an album that, as Alicia acknowledged, represented a **turbulent** time in her life. "[This album] made me have to tear down the walls, look at who I was, what I wanted, and what was important."

CRITICAL DARLING

Awards and critical acceptance were nothing new for Alicia. Since bursting onto the music scene in 2001 with her debut album *Songs in A Minor*, awards have become a way of life for the singer/songwriter from New York City. She has won fourteen Grammy awards and countless other musical awards. She has sold over thirty million albums worldwide.

Critics responded positively to Alicia's obvious fondness and respect for diverse musical styles, as well as the wisdom and understanding of life that marked her lyrics. As one reviewer remarked, "*Songs in A Minor* carries an old soul wisdom, **sagacity**, and heartache that belies her age." *Rolling Stone* magazine said that "Fallin'"—the most popular song from the album—"combines writing of Prince-ish complexity about the joy and pain of love with singing worthy of the soul giants." *Reader's Digest Australia*, whose reviewer felt that Alicia was an "old soul," asked her if she thought she had lived before. Alicia responded, "I think I have.... I feel I connect with the '30s and '40s. Maybe in some way I was alive then, and came back for this time now."

No matter what era Alicia Keys connects with, music fans are certainly glad she is here now. She has come a long way to get to the top. It's been a journey with more emotional twists and turns than a blues song.

A Child of Several Cultures

On January 25, 1981, in New York City, Terri Auguello and Craig Cook had a baby girl. Her name was Alicia Auguello Cook, and she would grow up on the city streets and one day become famous as Alicia Keys. (She changed her last name because of her fondness for the piano.)

A Big World of Everything

Craig was a flight attendant with black skin from Jamaica. An Italian American, Terri wanted to be an actress. Craig left Terri when Alicia was just two years old, and Terri took a job as a **paralegal** to help pay the bills. Alicia grew up

Alicia shares a fashionable moment with her grandmother and mother. She was raised in a biracial family in a multicultural neighborhood and had friends from many ethnic groups. Early on she experienced a variety of musical styles, especially in the New York neighborhood of Harlem.

on 43rd Street and 10th Avenue in Manhattan, in a rough neighborhood called Hell's Kitchen. Alicia told *Reader's Digest* that it was a world of opposites.

"It was like a big world of everything. I grew up around prostitutes, drug dealers, pimps, strippers, [and] needles on the ground. Yet right there was Broadway, with the big lights and Theater Row. [It was] a place that from the beginning told me you can go this way—or you can go that way."

Growing up, Alicia had friends in many different racial and ethnic groups. One place she felt particularly comfortable was Harlem. Harlem taught her the street skills she needed to survive in the city. The neighborhood's rich musical history allowed Alicia to experience many different types of music, from Marvin Gaye to Jimi Hendrix.

Like the Wind

Mariah Carey is another famous female musician who is the product of a biracial marriage. She was born March 27, 1970, and is named after the song "They Call the Wind Mariah."

Mariah's mother Patricia was Irish, and her father Alfred was Afro-Venezuelan. The couple had difficulties getting along and divorced when Mariah was four. Like Alicia's mother, Mariah's mother worked multiple jobs to pay the bills. She was a vocal coach and began teaching Mariah how to sing at age three.

At a party in 1988, Mariah met Tommy Mottola of Columbia Records. He signed a contract with her (they eventually married, then divorced), and she went on to become Columbia's highest-selling artist.

Growing up, Alicia saw the contrasts between poverty on the streets and the musical and cultural opportunities New York had to offer. She noted that she had the choice of going in one direction or the other. She chose music.

MUSICAL UPBRINGING

Alicia's first piano was a 1920s player piano she got when a friend moved. She wrote her first songs on it. Alicia told *Reader's Digest Australia* that arguing with her mother helped her learn to write: "[We'd] have these crazy, crazy fights. Everyone would storm out mad, and the only way that I'd be able to express myself was to write her."

Alicia wrote her first song after seeing the movie *Philadelphia*. Her grandfather had died the previous year, and her emotional **turmoil** poured into the song "I'm All Alone."

Alicia was determined to play the piano well. She always loved the sound and feel of the instrument. She studied classical music from age six to eighteen, practicing six hours a day. Alicia told *Reader's Digest* that once she told her mother she wanted to stop playing the piano. Terri told her to take a break—but that was it. Alicia later wondered, "Now I wonder if she hadn't told me that, who would I be?"

BABY GRAND

When Alicia was twelve years old in 1993, she was accepted at the Professional Performing Arts School in New York City. She thrived in this artist-friendly environment, taking classes in dance, theater, and music.

A man named Conrad Robinson started giving Alicia vocal lessons at the Harlem Police Athletic League. He begged his brother Jeff, a manager of singers, to come and watch Alicia perform. After running out of excuses, Jeff finally went. He was impressed when he heard Alicia sing—but he was blown away when he heard her play piano. He became her manager.

Alicia already knew the dangers of rushing into a recording deal. When she was about sixteen, a record company executive had brought her into a room with a beautiful white baby grand piano. Promised the piano, Alicia signed, but the deal turned sour. As she joked to *Reader's Digest Australia*, "[The] moral of the story is never sign a contract for a baby grand piano!"

MEETING CLIVE DAVIS

Jeff Robinson set up a showcase for Alicia's talents among record industry people, knowing that her natural abilities would shine. Columbia Records signed her for $400,000, but again, the deal went bad. Columbia wanted her to just sing and be a pop princess and let others produce the music. Alicia wanted to make music that stirred her soul—and she wanted to produce her own albums. She recorded just one song with Columbia, "Dah Dee Dah (Sexy Thing)," which appeared on the *Men in Black* movie soundtrack.

Jeff stopped the recording sessions, set Alicia up with other producers so she could learn album production, and took her to see Clive Davis at Arista Records. Clive had launched the careers of Bruce Springsteen, Whitney Houston, and Billy Joel, among many others. He knew talent, and he knew Alicia had it. Clive told *Rolling Stone*, "I knew she was unique."

Clive bought out her Columbia contract and signed her, advising her to be herself. Things finally seemed on track for Alicia.

CHAPTER
3

TO THE TOP

Once Alicia released her first album, *Songs in A Minor*, in 2001, she began a steady climb to the top of the musical world. The album was an immediate hit with critics and fans alike and won numerous awards. It meant the arrival of a new and talented voice on the music scene.

J RECORDS

After Alicia left Columbia and signed with Clive and Arista Records, it seemed like her path was smoothing out, something that she needed after such a long period of uncer-

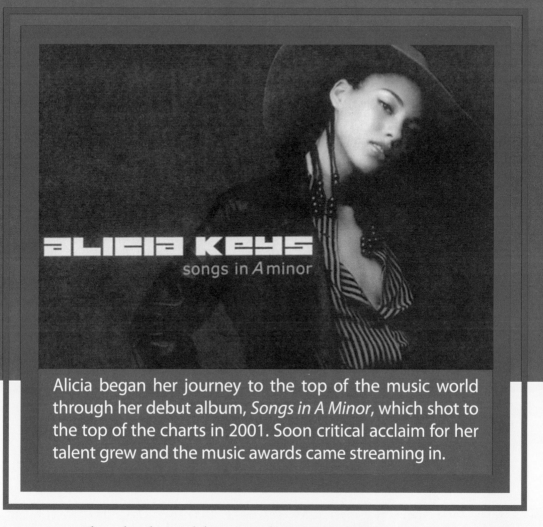

Alicia began her journey to the top of the music world through her debut album, *Songs in A Minor*, which shot to the top of the charts in 2001. Soon critical acclaim for her talent grew and the music awards came streaming in.

tainty. Clive had a golden touch in nurturing new talent and a reputation for letting new artists find their voices.

So it must have come as something of a shock to Alicia when Clive abruptly left Arista Records. Was the disaster with Columbia about to be repeated? Did Clive's leaving mean that Alicia's career was to be left in the hands of other music executives who did not understand her the same way he did? Fortunately, the answer was no. Clive decided to

Clive Davis and Alicia enjoy the success of her first album. Clive founded J Records and developed a strategy to showcase Alicia's classical training on TV before her album was released. His plan worked well, and after several TV appearances Alicia and *Songs in A Minor* were on their way.

start his own company called J Records, and he took Alicia with him to his new label. As he later told *Rolling Stone*, he knew that the young girl from Hell's Kitchen was something extraordinary. "Did I know she was going to sell a million records? Of course not! . . . I knew she was special, I knew she was a self-contained artist."

CREATING A BUZZ

Clive founded J Records in 2000. It took him some time before he could get the company established and ready to release records by its artists. So Alicia, who had waited so long for the opportunity to record an album of her own music, had to wait a bit longer. By 2001 Clive was ready. Typically, new artists are introduced to the public through the radio and MTV by a hit song. However, Clive knew that this strategy would not work for Alicia. She was a classically trained pianist with a unique style. The song "Fallin'" began with classical music by Chopin. Clearly, Alicia wasn't a typical pop musician, so the typical ways to introduce her to audiences would not be effective.

Clive knew just what to do. He decided to showcase her talents and start creating a buzz. As he said, "Few new artists can be showcased this way and blow people away. But she can cause a hurricane on stage. So we showcased her for tastemakers." Ironically, considering the ultimate popularity of Alicia's first album, Clive had to call upon all his considerable skill and experience just to get the record and Alicia established.

Bursting Out

Clive used many different methods to get Alicia into the public view. At one of his showcases, a talent scout for *The Tonight Show* was so impressed that Alicia was immediately booked for the show. Clive personally took the video for "Fallin'" to MTV, where it was an instant sensation. Finally, he wrote a personal letter to Oprah Winfrey. He told her she should do the same thing for music that she did for authors—feature new talent on her program. The day after his letter reached Oprah, Clive received a call about Alicia—she was going to be on Oprah's show. Clive's strategy had worked like a charm. Alicia appeared on *The Tonight Show* and *The Oprah Winfrey Show*. The video for "Fallin'" was a buzz clip on MTV. All of this built up incredible anticipation for the release of Alicia's album.

When the album, *Songs in A Minor*, was finally released on June 5, 2001, it took the music industry by storm. The album sold 236,000 copies in its first week and debuted at number one on the *Billboard* 200. By the second week, requests for the disc were so numerous that record stores ordered another 450,000 copies of the album. Alicia was on her way. As Clive pointed out, Alicia was her own goodwill ambassador.

Grammy Girl

Songs in A Minor continued its strong performance throughout 2001. *Rolling Stone* ranked it second on its list of top-ten albums of 2001. It was also included on *Q* magazine's list of the 100 Greatest Albums Ever.

It didn't take long for the awards and recognition to start coming in. Alicia won the MTV Video Music Award for Best New Artist. She won two *Billboard* awards: Female New Artist of the Year and Hip-Hop New Artist of the Year. She performed at a fundraiser aired on television for victims of the 9/11 terrorist attacks. The season premiere of the popular television show *Saturday Night Live* featured Alicia. She was on the cover of *Rolling Stone*.

Alicia received a huge honor in February 2002. She won a record-tying five Grammy Awards. She won for Best New Artist, Song of the Year ("Fallin'"), Best R&B Album, Best R&B Song ("Fallin'"), and Best Female R&B Vocal Performance. Alicia later revealed to *People* magazine that she was ill during her big night at the Grammys—and it wasn't from nerves!

"I was sick with a cold. It was a mixture between a sick fog and a dream fog. I sat down and I looked to my right and there was Bono and Céline Dion. Brian McKnight was in front of me. I said, 'Whoa, what am I doing here?'"

As her five Grammys proved, Alicia certainly did belong with music's best.

Five Times the Fun

When Alicia won five Grammy Awards at the 2002 awards show, it marked only the second time in the history of the Grammy Awards that a woman had won five Grammys in the same year.

Lauryn Hill was the first, winning five in 1999 for her album *The Miseducation of Lauryn Hill*. Since Alicia's wins, however, women have won five Grammys so often that it's now almost routine.

ONE-HIT WONDER
OR SOPHOMORE STAR?

The year 2002 only added to Alicia's popularity and growing list of awards. BET named her Best New Artist. She won two Soul Train Music awards, a Soul Train Lady of Soul Award, and many others. She went on a successful concert tour. *Songs in A Minor* was a certifiable smash. Then it was time to do it all again.

The music industry has a term for artists who explode onto the scene with a hit, only to never be heard from again: one-

Alicia dazzles an audience with her sultry voice in 2003. Her sophomore album, *The Diary of Alicia Keys*, was her second to shoot immediately to number one on the *Billboard* 200.

hit wonders. Some people wondered if that was going to be Alicia's fate. On its cover, *Pride* magazine asked if Alicia could avoid the dreaded "sophomore jinx." Then she released her second album, *The Diary of Alicia Keys*, and it was quickly evident that Alicia was going to be around for a while.

The Diary of Alicia Keys was released on December 2, 2003. It sold more than 618,000 copies its first week. In so doing, it became Alicia's second consecutive album to debut at number one on the *Billboard* 200. The critics once again raved about the work. Typical of the critical reaction was MSN Music, which said that *The Diary of Alicia Keys* emphasized Alicia's sexy, sultry voice and her inner soulfulness.

Sophomore Slump

The sophomore slump, or sophomore jinx, is a term used to refer to second-year efforts that are not as good or as notable as the first one.

In sports, it is often common for players who are unfamiliar to opponents in their first year to become known by their second. Thus teams are prepared for the player, and his or her achievements are not as spectacular as they were previously. In entertainment, particularly music, artists have years to craft songs for their first album. Once it comes out and they are popular, however, the pressures of touring and fame often cause their second effort to be mediocre at best because they have little time to recreate the magic.

Hit Singles and Awards

Diary spawned four hit singles: "You Don't Know My Name," "If I Ain't Got You," "Diary," and "Karma." All these songs made the *Billboard* Top 20. However, one of Alicia's most popular songs wasn't even included on the *Diary* album. It was called "My Boo," and it was a duet with male R&B artist Usher. It was included on Usher's 2004 album *Confessions*. The song hit number one on the *Billboard* Top 100. Usher was the only solo R&B artist in 2004 to sell more records than Alicia.

It turned out to be another year of awards for Alicia. Among them were the Best R&B Video at the MTV Video Music Awards, songwriter of the year at the African American Literary Awards, and NAACP (National Association for the Advancement of Colored People) Award for Best Female Artist.

The 2004 MTV Video Awards, held in August in Miami, were a particularly memorable night for Alicia. Both Stevie Wonder and Lenny Kravitz came on stage to join Alicia in performing her song "If I Ain't Got You." That night Alicia also paid tribute to the legendary Ray Charles.

Keep a Child Alive

But there was more to this young superstar from Hell's Kitchen than just hit records and awards—much more. Her charity efforts began in 2002 when she had gone to Africa for a concert. Driving in from the airport, Alicia saw the

ramshackle shantytowns next to lush golf courses. She also met kids younger than she was who were HIV-positive and didn't have any parents. As she told *Marie Claire* magazine, everything hit her at breakfast.

"Right after that, I went on vacation in the Seychelles islands; it was all sexy and amazing, and I ordered breakfast—eggs and orange juice—and it came to $85. I was like, Whoa! That smacked me so hard in the face. I knew I wanted to do something."

Within a year Alicia had co-founded the organization Keep A Child Alive with Leigh Blake. Leigh had a long history of battling **AIDS**, dating back to co-founding the Red Hot Organization in the late 1980s. Keep A Child Alive began helping to build clinics and also provide medicine for African children and their families with AIDS.

Alicia had been involved previously in raising money to combat AIDS. On December 12, 2001, she had performed at "The Concert—20 Years of AIDS" in Los Angeles. The concert, headlined by Elton John and featuring Bon Jovi, Sting, and others, was held to raise money for AIDS Project Los Angeles and the Elton John AIDS Foundation. Now with Keep A Child Alive, Alicia had moved her commitment to fighting this disease to a whole new level.

ALICIA KEYS, AUTHOR

Later in 2004, Alicia moved to conquer another area in entertainment: writing. She released a book that combined her lyrics from her first two albums with some of her unpublished poems. She called the book *Tears for Water*. In the book's introduction, she explained why: "I call this *Tears for Water* because in looking through all these words I have come to the understanding that everything I have ever written has stemmed from my tears of joy, of pain, of sorrow, of depression, and of question."

The book would go on to make the *New York Times* bestseller list in 2005. Between the success of the book, touring, and her album sales, *Rolling Stone* estimated that Alicia made $10 million in 2004.

KRUCIALKEYS

Alicia also proved that she was no slouch in the business department. While she was working on her first album, *Songs in A Minor*, Alicia formed a production company with songwriter and record producer Kerry Brothers, Jr., who helped Alicia write and produce the album. He co-wrote several of the album's tracks, among them "Troubles" and "Rock wit U." He is known as "K" or "Krucial," so the company was called KrucialKeys.

As Kerry later told *Boxxet*, the two worked so well together that it seemed to make sense for them to join forces in a business sense: "During the first album, we formed a production company by the name of KrucialKeys…When you look at history and see the success of teams like us, it only made sense for us to combine and always continue."

Alicia shares a keen business sense with Kerry "Krucial" Brothers, who helped write some tracks on her first album. They founded a production company and have been successful partners ever since. Although rumors have linked the pair romantically, Alicia has explained they are not a couple.

The history of the music industry is filled with stories of artists who were great singers and songwriters but poor business people. They made little money on their fame and success, and once they couldn't produce anymore they faded into **obscurity** and poverty. By moving to create a business partnership with someone instrumental to her success, Alicia was determined not to let that happen to her.

4

THE BEAT GOES ON

By the year 2005, few artists in the world were more successful than Alicia. She had sold millions of records, won numerous awards, and written a best-selling book. In an era when musicians burst onto the horizon only to quickly fade away, Alicia had only become more popular since her debut album *Songs in A Minor*.

GOOD BEGINNING

Alicia started 2005 on a good note. At the forty-seventh annual Grammy Awards on February 13, she won four more Gram-

Alicia keeps the beat going in a recording studio. Her hard work paid off again in 2005, when she won four more Grammys. That year she also appeared in benefit concerts, released an acoustic album, and won several more music awards.

mys: Best Female R&B Vocal Performance for "If I Ain't Got You," Best R&B Song for "You Don't Know My Name," Best R&B Album for *The Diary of Alicia Keys*, and Best R&B Performance by a Duo or Group with Vocals for "My Boo," the song she had performed with Usher on his 2004 album *Confessions*.

In addition, at the Grammy show Alicia had joined Jamie Foxx and Quincy Jones to perform the classic song Ray

Charles had made famous called "Georgia on My Mind." It was another example of how effortlessly Alicia can move through different styles of music. As she told one magazine, she had always been good at switching between musical worlds.

On July 2, 2005, Alicia appeared at the Live 8 Concert in Philadelphia along with a star-studded lineup that included Will Smith, the Black-Eyed Peas, and Stevie Wonder. The concert was held in front of the Philadelphia Art Museum. Hundreds of thousands of people in attendance and millions more on television saw Alicia perform the song "For All We Know."

Live 8

Live 8 was a series of benefit concerts held throughout the world on July 2, 2005. A primary goal of the concerts was to pressure the upcoming meeting of the G8 countries (Canada, France, Germany, Italy, Japan, Russia, the United Kingdom, and the United States) into lowering the financial debt owned by the world's poorer nations, many of which are in Africa.

The hope was that these needy countries could then use that money to help improve conditions for their citizens.

Ten concerts were held on July 2, watched by an estimated three billion people. A few days later, the G8 nations pledged to double aid levels to poorer nations by 2010. Half of that money was slated for Africa.

UNPLUGGING

MTV's *Unplugged* show was a groundbreaking and award-winning affair in the 1990s that spotlighted artists performing without the aid of electrical amplification. In 2005, MTV wanted to revive the show, and they asked Alicia to appear in the first segment. In July, she filmed her appearance at the Brooklyn Academy of Music, with guests Common, Mos Def, and others. Alicia performed many of her songs—with new arrangements—and continued to demonstrate her easy acceptance and appreciation of different musical styles by covering older songs like the Rolling Stones' "Wild Horses."

In October, Alicia released the album *Unplugged*, based on her performance on the show. The record exploded out of the starting gate just like her first two, debuting as number one on the *Billboard* 200. It sold nearly 200,000 copies in the United States in the first week and close to 250,000 copies worldwide. It was the first "unplugged" album by a female artist to debut at number one.

In an interview in *Billboard*, Alicia discussed why her music fit the unplugged format so well: "Before I even got signed, I'd play these small clubs . . . me on the piano, playing a couple of songs I'd written and talking to the people in between. The smaller you strip things down, the more you depend on the songs and yourself, as opposed to arrangements. To go back to this style is one of the reasons why I really wanted to do this 'Unplugged.'"

"UNBREAKABLE"

Alicia revealed that the first single from the album, "Unbreakable," had originally been intended for her previous album *The Diary of Alicia Keys*, but it hadn't seemed to fit. However, she thought the style of the song was perfect for the unplugged format, so she decided to include it in the album. As always, Alicia's musical instincts were right. "Unbreakable" would go on to remain at number one on the *Billboard*

Alicia gives a soulful performance in 2005. That year her single, "Unbreakable," became a number-one hit. But rather than rest on her many awards, she continued her charity work, including benefits for hurricane and tsunami victims. Alicia has said she always believes in the healing power of music.

Hot Adult R&B Airplay chart for eleven weeks. Awards for Alicia mounted up again in 2005. Besides her Grammys, she also won the People's Choice Award as the Favorite Female Artist, an NAACP Image Award, a BET Award for Best R&B Female Artist, multiple Soul Train Awards, and several ASCAP Rhythm and Soul Awards.

THE POWER OF MUSIC

All the honors and awards only seemed to ramp up Alicia's charity work. After Hurricane Katrina devastated the Gulf Coast of the United States in the summer of 2005, Alicia performed at several events to help raise money for storm victims. She also helped to raise money for **tsunami** relief efforts in Southeast Asia. Besides the goal of fund-raising, the performances reflected Alicia's belief in the healing power of music. She said, "I feel that music has a way of reaching people and joining people in a way that not many other things can. [After Katrina] music was the driving force that made people say, 'Wow, I have to get involved.'"

Alicia's commitment to working for others is considerable. She uses the power of her music for good by working with the Hip-Hop Summit Action Network, which seeks to harness the power of hip-hop for the benefit of African American youths. Other charities that benefit from Alicia's tireless commitment to making the world a better place include Frum Tha Ground Up and Teens in Motion.

Fighting AIDS

Always uppermost in Alicia's mind is the fight against AIDS. She and Bono recorded a version of the song "Don't Give Up," renamed "Don't Give Up (Africa)," for World AIDS Day. An exclusive ringtone was developed from that song by Cingular, which donated all the proceeds from its sale to Keep A Child Alive.

In April 2006, she traveled to Kenya and Uganda to visit children's HIV clinics and other services to try and raise awareness about the special needs of children with the disease.

In August, 2006, Alicia addressed the sixteenth Annual AIDS Conference in Toronto, Canada: "We must come together . . . and fight for the rights of children and families suffering from this dreadful disease. We must never give up . . . until we can stand together and say, 'We did not sit idly by and watch an entire continent perish.'"

Charitable Celebrities

Like Alicia, a great number of celebrities believe they can use their substantial star power to make the world a better place for others.

Bono of U2 is one example. He has worked with DATA (Debt Aids Trade Africa), helped organize Live 8, donated money to One in Four Ireland (a charity for Irish sexual abuse victims), and assisted numerous other causes. He has been nominated for three Nobel Peace Prizes.

Many entertainers work for the benefit of others: Julia Roberts works with The Hole In the Wall Gang, Morgan Freeman established the Grenada Relief Fund, and Matt Damon started H2O Africa. These and many more celebrities are unselfish ambassadors for doing good.

LIGHTS, CAMERA, ACTION!

In October 2005, it was announced that Alicia was to appear in her first film role. It was a movie called *Smokin' Aces*, with Alicia playing an assassin named Georgia Sykes. Co-star Jeremy Piven told MTV.com he was confident that Alicia would have no trouble as an actress. He explained that anyone who can consistently perform at a high level like Alicia should hit a home run in acting.

Alicia followed *Smokin' Aces* with a role in *The Nanny Diaries*, playing a best friend.

SOMETHING WRONG

While she was filming *Smokin' Aces* and *The Nanny Diaries*, Alicia felt like something was wrong—not physically, but emotionally. She had been going virtually nonstop since first emerging onto the scene—touring, charity events, and promotional appearances—and she was worn down. As she told *Entertainment Weekly*, "I would look in the mirror and I didn't know who that person was."

Her increasingly hectic schedule, particularly filming movies, was pulling Alicia apart. She found herself shooting the movie twelve hours a day, then hurrying to the studio to record her music. She would stay there until late in the evening, grab a few hours sleep, and then be back on the movie set. Alicia became a slave to her schedule, and she moved mechanically from appointment to appointment. Her long-time best friend Erika Rose grew increasingly worried that the special spark that burned inside Alicia was in danger of being snuffed out.

The music that came out of her during this time reflected her distorted sense of self. Manager Jeff Robinson said that the songs she wrote now were dark and odd—not like Alicia's usual music.

To a Head

Things came to a head in the summer of 2006. Her grandmother, with whom she was very close, was diagnosed with cancer. Alicia visited her every Sunday and took care of all the medical expenses. More importantly, she told *Entertainment Weekly* that the illness made her finally get off the spinning merry-go-round she was on and take stock of her own life. "It made me finally stop. Nothing else was more important—no work, no costumes, no anything. I was forced to slow down, look at my life, and decide who I wanted to be."

Her grandmother's death in September made Alicia realize that things had to change. She fled to Egypt for a month-long vacation accompanied only by a local tour guide—no schedules and no commitments. When she returned she was renewed, refreshed, and refocused. Out of her newfound sense of self and security came the words and music for her next album: *As I Am*.

A Personal Record

Not only were the music and lyrics of *As I Am* more personal than anything Alicia had ever done before, but her singing style was also more intense and emotional. As she told *Entertainment Weekly*, "This CD was so severely personal, it changed my voice. There's so much more that I needed to say."

Alicia told *Flare* that each of her albums marks a certain period in her life, and a new awareness of her events and surroundings. With her second album, it was awareness of the world. With *As I Am*, Alicia looked inward. The record was a journey of self-awareness.

CHANGING HER APPEARANCE

Alicia not only changed her singing style but her image as well. Previously, she had styled her hair in cornrows and worn baggy jeans. It had been part of her attempt to build walls between herself and others. But now the cornrows and jeans were replaced by long, flowing hair and fashionable outfits. Alicia said, "Before, I was so much more closed. I wasn't comfortable in my own skin. I'm still being myself, but now, I'm more open to exploring different sides of me."

Changing image and appearance can be risky for a celebrity. How would Alicia's fans react?

MORE TO GO

The phenomenal reception to *As I Am* quickly erased any doubts about whether Alicia's fans would accept her new sound and appearance. She was more popular than ever, and now increasingly showed that there was much more to her than just a hit album.

AROUND THE WORLD

First on Alicia's 2008 agenda was an international tour in support of *As I Am*. Millions of fans around the world had bought the record and were anxious to see Alicia perform in

Alicia struts her stuff during her *As I Am* tour in 2008. The tour offered fans worldwide the chance to see Alicia's unique style. She said she wanted to keep the fans energized but also give the concerts an intimate feeling—as though she could bring fans into her world.

person. To accommodate them all, Alicia scheduled a tour that went on throughout all of 2008. The tour zigzagged across the globe.

During one of her stops in the United States, Alicia talked with *USA Today* about her show: "I decided to make the show like a journey, from the beginning to where I am now. I love performing in theaters, because it's so close-knit; I can see everybody and get a vibe going. I wanted to be able to translate that feeling to a larger venue—to bring you into my world, but also provide excitement."

Alicia toured Europe, visiting England, France, Germany, Switzerland, Spain, and Portugal. In Asia, she performed in China, Japan, Indonesia, South Korea, the Philippines, and Singapore. She even found time to visit Australia and New Zealand. By the time the tour ended in late December 2008, it was estimated to have grossed over $22 million. Hundreds of thousands of people around the world had gone to see Alicia's high-energy act.

Reviews of Alicia's shows were positive. The British newspaper *Manchester Evening News* said that Alicia's extreme dignity, teamed with her ability to both silence and excite her audience through her performance at the piano, secured her place among modern R&B royalty.

FILM AND TV PROJECTS

Although the *As I Am* world tour was long and comprehensive, Alicia somehow found time to participate in numerous other projects during the year. She starred in a "micro" television series called *Fresh Takes*, which was created by Dove to promote their Go Fresh products. The three-minute segments, which aired during MTV's *The Hills*, traced the pressures of a group of women in their 20s—an age bracket to which Alicia certainly could relate. As she said to *USA Today*, "People of my generation are such overachievers. There's a stress level, and I've dealt with that, being a hard worker and someone who wants to accomplish a lot of things."

In October 2008, Alicia's third film, *The Secret Life of Bees*, premiered. Alicia played June Boatwright, one of three sisters who harvest and bottle honey. Alicia talked to *USA Today* about how complicated the character was, and how the film role was one of the best things she had been involved with yet. She enjoyed the fact that during the film the character finds a way to be more open and comfortable with who she is, and becomes less afraid of life and love.

Alicia (second from right) poses with the cast of *The Secret Life of Bees*. She enjoyed her third film role as a complex woman who becomes more open to life as the film progresses. Alicia's work earned her an NAACP Image Award nomination for Outstanding Supporting Actress in a Motion Picture.

COVER GIRL

Although Alicia was used to having her picture in magazines because of all her musical achievements and awards, her new, more glamorous look caused her to be sought after for magazine photo shoots and stories. Everybody wanted to showcase her new style. The magazine *Flare* stated that Alicia's look had now changed from "ghetto fabulous" to "extraordinarily fabulous."

POLITICAL POWER

In 2008, Alicia put the power of her growing fame into action in another arena: politics. She endorsed Barack Obama for president. She felt strongly that Obama was a person who could connect to everyone and that this would contribute for the good of the country. He seemed to be reaching all racial and ethnic groups.

After winning the Democratic presidential nomination, Obama went on to win the election in November 2008. When he was sworn into office on January 20, 2009, Alicia and her mother Terri were among the thousands of spectators who braved the cold weather in Washington, D.C., to watch him take the oath of office.

That night, Alicia performed at the Neighborhood Ball as part of the inauguration festivities. Other entertainers at the ball included Sting, Mariah Carey, Beyoncé, Faith Hill, and Stevie Wonder. Alicia sang her hit song "No One," and she also participated in all all-star group rendition of Stevie Wonder's classic "Signed, Sealed, Delivered, I'm Yours."

Later, in an entry on MTV.com, Alicia talked about her feelings concerning the inauguration, "I didn't care how cold it was or how far I had to walk, it was a must for me to attend the inauguration! The pulse of the people was alive and beating! Everyone knew this was that moment, which from this day forward will never be forgotten."

Two months later, Alicia had an opportunity to again use the power of her fame in the political world. On March 19 she, along with a number of other celebrities, journeyed to

First lady Michelle Obama (left) meets Alicia and BET executive Debra Lee at the White House during the kickoff celebration of Women's History Month in 2009. Twenty-one women at the top of their fields joined the first lady in visiting local schools and speaking with students about their career goals.

Washington, D.C., to speak at area high schools in support of Women's History Month. Alicia spoke at Dunbar High School in Washington. A special highlight of that day for Alicia was meeting the new First Lady of the United States, Michelle Obama.

Women's History Month

Until the 1960s, history had largely been the story of men and what they had done. The contributions and achievements of women were ignored. But beginning in the 1960s, it was recognized that women had played a key role in many famous events and eras in America.

The first celebration of women in history began in 1978 in Sonoma County, California. It was called "Women's History Week," and was held so that it included March 8, International Women's Day. The event quickly proved to be popular. In 1981 U.S. Senator Orrin Hatch and Representative Barbara Mikulski co-sponsored a resolution making Women's History Week a national event. In 1987, the U.S. Congress designated the entire month of March as Women's History Month.

MORE AWARDS FOR *AS I AM*

Alicia's album *As I Am* continued to shine throughout 2008. Early in the year it won the NAACP award as Outstanding Album. The song "Like You'll Never See Me Again" won awards for Outstanding Music Video and Outstanding Song. At the American Music Awards in November, it won

Favorite Album in both the Pop/Rock and Soul, Rhythm & Blues categories.

In November 2008, *As I Am* was re-released in the United States and elsewhere in a Super Edition version. It contained five new songs as well as a bonus disc of Alicia performing five songs live at the Coronet Theater in London, England.

ALICIA IN AFRICA

Alicia is the Global Ambassador for Keep A Child Alive. She is the face of the organization. At a concert, she raised $40,000 for the charity on the spot by urging fans to donate $5. She journeyed to Uganda, South Africa, and Kenya for a month to visit AIDS-stricken communities. She posted a documentary on the Internet about the trip and called it *Alicia in Africa*. Talking about Keep A Child Alive, Alicia told *Marie Claire*, "This organization has so much heart and truth and honesty and integrity. It's genuine and personal. It helps me be clear on things that are way bigger than the walls we have around us."

THE FUTURE IS NOW

Alicia has accomplished many amazing things since bursting onto the scene in 2001 and taking the entertainment industry—as well as the world—by storm. Yet it seems as if she's just getting warmed up.

In the summer of 2005, Alicia and her KrucialKeys Enterprises partner Kerry "Krucial" Brothers opened a new state-of-the-art recording studio in Long Island, New York, called Oven Studios. One of the people involved in the design was also involved in legendary guitarist Jimi Hendrix's Electric Ladyland Studios.

Alicia and manager Jeff Robinson are developing several television and movie projects. Among them are a show based on Alicia's childhood about a biracial fifteen-year-old growing up and a remake of the classic film *Bell, Book, and Candle*. Alicia has also been announced to star in *Composition in Black and White*, a film about African American child prodigy pianist Philippa Schuyler. Alicia spoke about how people like Barbra Streisand and Quincy Jones were her role models because of the way they can act and perform music.

More to Go

Alicia's success has continued throughout recent years. She worked with Jay-Z on the song "Empire State of Mind" that topped the *Billboard* Hot 100. Alicia and Jay-Z won two Grammys for "Empire State of Mind," for Best Rap/Sung Collaboration and Best Rap Song. She worked with recording artist Alejandro Sanz on the song "Looking for Paradise," which topped the Hot Latin Songs chart.

Alicia released her fourth album, *The Element of Freedom*, in December 2009. The album reached number two on the *Billboard* 200. *Billboard* magazine ranked her as the top R&B artist of 2000-2009 and the number-five artist of the decade.

In May 2010, Alicia and record producer Swizz Beatz announced both their engagement and that they would soon be having a child. They were married on July 31, 2010, and Alicia gave birth to a son, Egypt, on October 14.

In 2011, *Song in A Minor* was re-released in honor of its tenth anniversary and Alicia made her debut as a director of a documentary, *Five*, on the stories of five women with breast cancer. RCA Music Group also announced that J Records, Arista Records, and Jive Records were all shutting down. Because of this, Alicia will be releasing her future music with RCA Records.

Alicia Keys has accomplished more in a few short years than most people do in a lifetime—hit albums, charity work, awards, films, concerts worldwide, and numerous business ventures. It seems there's little that Alicia hasn't done. As she made clear to *Flare*, she has many hopes and dreams for the future.

"I have plenty more to go."

Alicia has achieved so much in so many fields that it is hard to predict what she will do next. With television and movie projects in the works and plans for future albums, the award-winning Alicia has her pick of whatever dreams she wants to pursue.

1981	Alicia Auguello Cook is born to Terri Auguello, an Italian American, and Craig Cook, an African American from Jamaica, in New York City on January 25.
1983	Parents divorce.
1985	At age four, Alicia gets a part in a *Cosby Show* episode, as one of the sleep-over friends of Rudy Huxtable.
1988	Alicia begins playing the piano.
1993	At age 12, Alicia is accepted at the Professional Performing Arts School in NYC.
1997	Alicia is accepted at Columbia University. Alicia signs with Columbia Records.
1999	Alicia leaves Columbia over creative differences and signs with Arista Records and Clive Davis.
2000	Clive Davis founds J Records after leaving Arista, and he takes Alicia with him.
2001	Alicia releases her debut album entitled *Songs in A Minor* on Davis's new label, J Records. The album sells 236,000 copies in its first week of release.
2002	Alicia wins five Grammy Awards, only the second woman at the time to do so.
2003	Alicia releases her second album, *The Diary of Alicia Keys*. It sells over 618,000 copies in its first week.
2004	Alicia writes a book entitled *Tears For Water: Songbook of Poems and Lyrics*.
2005	Alicia's book makes the *New York Times* Best Seller list. Alicia wins four more Grammy Awards. Alicia releases her first live album entitled *Unplugged*.

Alicia and Bono, lead singer for the rock band U2, record a cover version of the song "Don't Give Up" in recognition of World AIDS Day.

2006 Alicia makes her film debut in the movie *Smokin' Aces*, playing an assassin.

2007 Alicia appears in her second movie, *The Nanny Diaries*. This time, she plays a more traditional role as a best friend.

Alicia releases her third studio album, *As I Am*. It sells 742,000 copies in its first week.

2008 Alicia wins two more Grammy Awards.

Alicia stars in *Fresh Takes*, a commercial micro-series created by Dove products, which premiered during *The Hills* on MTV.

The documentary film *Alicia in Africa: Journey to the Motherland* is released and available on the Internet. It is a movie about Alicia's trip to Africa on behalf of AIDS victims.

Alicia appears in her third film, *The Secret Life of Bees*, playing one of the bee-raising sisters.

2009 Alicia attends the inauguration of President Barack Obama in Washington, D.C.

Alicia wins one more Grammy Award.

Alicia releases her fourth album *The Element of Freedom*.

2010 Alicia marries Swizz Beatz.

Alicia and Swizz Beatz have a son named Egypt.

2011 Alicia directs *Five*, a documentary on the lives of five women with breast cancer.

Albums

2001	*Songs in A Minor*
2003	*The Diary of Alicia Keys*
2005	*Unplugged*
2007	*As I Am*
2009	*The Element of Freedom*

Number-one Singles

2001	"Fallin'"
2004	"My Boo" (with Usher)
2007	"No One"

Book

2004	*Tears for Water*

Films

2007	*Smokin' Aces*
2007	*The Nanny Diaries*
2008	*The Secret Life of Bees*

Selected Awards

2001   *Billboard* Music Awards; MTV Video Music Award.

2002   American Music Award; BET Award; *Billboard* R&B/Hip-Hop Awards; Echo Award; Five Grammy Awards; MTV Europe Music Award; NAACP Image Awards; Soul Train Music Awards; Soul Train Lady of Soul Award; World Music Award.

2004   American Music Award; *Billboard* Music Awards; MTV Video Music Award; MTV Europe Music Award; Vibe Awards.

2005   ASCAP Pop Awards; ASCAP Rhythm & Soul Awards; BET Award; *Billboard* R&B/Hip-Hop Awards; Four Grammy Awards; MTV Video Music Award; MTV Europe Music Award; NAACP Image Award; People's Choice award; Soul Train Music Awards.

2006   NAACP Image Awards.

2008   American Music Award; BET Award; BET J Virtual Award; Two Grammy Awards; MTV Africa Music Award; NAACP Image Awards; Satellite Award; Swiss Music Award; World Music Award.

2009   ASCAP Pop Award; People's Choice Award; Two Grammy Awards.

AIDS—a deadly disease caused by a virus that attacks a person's ability to fight germs.

genres—categories of music with a certain style or theme (for example, rhythm and blues or rock).

introspective—to look into or examine one's one mind, or feelings.

obscurity—of little or no notice.

paralegal—someone who assists a lawyer.

prestigious—having a high reputation.

ramshackle—rickety, falling apart.

sagacity—wisdom or perception.

tsunami—an unusually large ocean wave produced by a seaquake or undersea volcanic eruption.

turbulent—agitated; disturbed; unsettled.

turmoil—a state of great commotion, confusion, or disturbance.

Books

Chang, Jeff. *Can't Stop, Won't Stop: A History of the Hip-Hop Generation*. New York: St. Martin's Press, 2005.

Keys, Alicia. *Tears for Water: Songbook of Poems & Lyrics*. New York: G.P. Putnam's Sons, 2004.

Stacy-Deanne, Kelly Kenyatta, Natasha Lowery, and Kwynn Sanders. *Alicia Keys, Ashanti, Beyoncé, Destiny's Child, Jennifer Lopez & Mya: Divas of the New Millennium*. Phoenix, Arizona: Colossus Books, 2005.

Websites

www.aliciakeys.com
> This is the official website for Alicia Keys. It offers news, videos, music, a store, and much more.

www.keepachildalive.org
> Keep A Child alive is the organization co-founded by Alicia that is battling AIDS in Africa. This is the group's official website, which offers news and information on how you can help.

www.allhiphop.com
> Like hip-hop music and news about your favorite artists? This is one of the places to go for music reviews, videos, rumors, and more.

Picture Credits

1: Sbukley | Dreamstime.com

4: José Goulão/Pix Int'l

8: Daniel Raustadt | Dreamstime.com

11: Frazer Harrison/Getty Images

12: RCA Music/NMI

14: Uptown/NMI

19: Ronald Asadorian/Splash News

21: RCA Music/PRMS

25: RCA Music/NMI

26: Russ Einhorn/StarMax

30: NY Photo Press/iPhoto

35: Maria Ramirez/Fashion Wire Daily

37: RCA Music/PRMS

40: José Goulão/Pix Int'l

47: Daniel Gluskoter/UPI Photo

49: Fox Searchlight Pictures/NMI

51: Alex Wong/Getty Images

55: RCA Music/PRMS

Front Cover: Sbukley | Dreamstime.com

About The Author

Russell Roberts is a fulltime freelance writer from New Jersey. He has written 12 books of non-fiction for adults, including the best-selling *Down the Jersey Shore*. He has also written over three dozen nonfiction books for kids, as well as hundreds of articles, during his career of more than 25 years. He currently lives with his wife, daughter, and a cranky Calico cat named Rusti.